BEYOND THE

WHISTLE

THE WAYNE BARNES

STORY

WRITTEN BY
THELMA SMITH

Table of contents

Preface

In the dynamic world of rugby, where players are revered and coaches celebrated, few figures stand at the crossroads of the sport's pulse like Wayne Barnes. "Beyond the Whistle: The Wayne Barnes Story" is an exploration into the life and career of a man whose journey from the grassroots to the global stage has left an indelible mark on rugby union refereeing.

As the author of this narrative, my aim is to unravel the layers of Wayne Barnes' story, a story that goes beyond the confines of the playing field. Born on April 20, 1979, in Bream, Gloucestershire, Barnes' affinity for rugby began in the heart of a community deeply entrenched in the sport. From those early days, a passion for the game grew, laying the foundation for a journey that would see him become a respected and influential figure in rugby officiating.

This book dives into Barnes' formative years, exploring the confluence of his education and love for rugby. It unravels the threads of his progression through local matches, navigating the challenges and opportunities that ultimately propelled him to the forefront of English and international rugby refereeing.

At the heart of "Beyond the Whistle" are the notable matches and moments that defined Barnes' career. From the iconic 2007 Rugby World Cup quarterfinal to the contentious clashes in the 2015 Rugby World Cup, these pivotal instances not only shaped matches but sparked broader conversations about the role and impact of referees in the sport.

The narrative extends beyond the controversies, shedding light on Barnes' role in domestic competitions like the English Premiership and European club rugby, as well as his presence in international tournaments such as the Six Nations and the Rugby Championship. It explores the nuanced and dynamic nature of refereeing at the highest levels, where adaptability and composure become as essential as a sound understanding of the laws of the game.

As we journey through Barnes' story, "Beyond the Whistle" also delves into the influence he wielded on rugby union refereeing. His legacy is not just about decisions made on the pitch but the lasting impact on the next generation of referees who looked to him as a mentor and role model.

.

Background and Early Career

Wayne Barnes was born on 20 April 1979, in Bream, Gloucestershire, England. Growing up in the picturesque county of Gloucestershire, Barnes developed an early passion for rugby. His formative years were marked by a deep connection to the sport, and it soon became evident that he possessed not only a keen understanding of the game but also a natural affinity for its rules and dynamics.

Raised in a rugby-centric environment, Barnes' upbringing played a pivotal role in shaping his trajectory towards becoming a prominent figure in the world of rugby refereeing. The local rugby culture, combined with his inherent interest in the sport, laid the foundation for a career that would see him officiate at the highest echelons of international rugby.

Barnes' journey from a rugby enthusiast in Gloucestershire to a distinguished international rugby union referee is a testament to his dedication and understanding of the game. His roots in a rugby-centric community undoubtedly contributed to the development of the skills and knowledge that would later define his career on the field.

Wayne Barnes' illustrious career as a rugby union referee unfolds as a captivating narrative, defined by a deep-rooted passion for the game, unwavering commitment, and a steady ascent to the pinnacles of international officiating.

Barnes' journey into rugby began in the heart of a community that lived and breathed the sport. The early days of his career saw him navigating the local rugby landscape, where his acute understanding of the game's intricacies and his adept management of on-field dynamics quickly set him apart.

The transition to the English Premiership marked a significant chapter in Barnes' career, where he became a familiar face in the rigorous and highly competitive league. His performances in domestic competitions earned him recognition, laying the foundation for an ascent into the realm of European rugby.

Barnes' influence extended beyond national boundaries as he took charge of matches in prestigious European tournaments, including the Heineken Cup and the European Challenge Cup. His ability to navigate the complexities of top-tier club competitions underscored his growing reputation as a referee of exceptional caliber.

The zenith of Barnes' career found expression on the international stage. His officiating duties encompassed the Rugby World Cup, where he earned the trust to preside over the sport's most significant event. Additionally, he played a central role in the drama of the

Six Nations, the intensity of the Rugby Championship, and the challenges of the Pacific Nations Cup.

Throughout his career, Barnes was not merely a referee but a central figure in some of rugby's most memorable moments. His composed demeanor under pressure and authoritative decision-making showcased a referee attuned to the nuances of the game. Whether in the heat of a closely contested match or the spotlight of a high-stakes final, Barnes' presence on the field became synonymous with fairness and precision.

As Wayne Barnes bid farewell to active refereeing, he left behind a legacy that transcended the scores of matches he officiated. His impact resonates in the standards he set for refereeing excellence, contributing significantly to the broader narrative of rugby union. Beyond the final whistle, his career stands as a testament to the integral role referees play in upholding the spirit and integrity of the sport.

Referee career

Wayne Barnes' pivotal role in the English Premiership elevated him to a position of prominence within the rugby officiating landscape. His journey within the league not only showcased his adept handling of high-stakes encounters but also underscored his contribution to maintaining the integrity and flow of the game.

As Barnes stepped onto the hallowed grounds of English Premiership rugby, he entered a realm known for its intense competition and physicality. The league, a crucible for emerging talent and seasoned veterans alike, demanded a referee of exceptional skill and understanding — qualities that Barnes quickly demonstrated.

His early forays into Premiership matches established Barnes as a referee capable of navigating the intricate balance between enforcing the rules and allowing the game to unfold organically. Match after match, he earned the respect of players, coaches, and fans alike through his consistent application of the laws and a keen sense of game management.

One of the hallmarks of Barnes' role in the Premiership was his ability to officiate matches of varying intensity. From closely contested battles for crucial league points to the pressure-cooker atmosphere of playoffs, he remained a composed figure on the field. His decisions, often made in split-second moments, reflected a deep understanding of the game's nuances and an unwavering commitment to fairness.

The English Premiership, with its diverse mix of teams and playing styles, presented a unique challenge for referees. Barnes, however, embraced this challenge, adapting his officiating style to suit the demands of each encounter. His presence on the field became synonymous with a measured authority that added to the spectacle of Premiership rugby.

Beyond the technical aspects of refereeing, Barnes also played a crucial role in shaping the narrative of matches. His communication skills, both with players and fellow officials, contributed to the overall positive atmosphere on the field. This ability to manage the human element of the game added another layer to his effectiveness as a referee.

Wayne Barnes' role in the English Premiership went beyond merely enforcing the rules. It was about fostering an environment where the game could thrive, where players could showcase their skills, and where the essence of rugby could shine. His tenure in the Premiership served as a foundation for the international acclaim that would follow, marking him as a referee who not only understood the game but also enhanced its essence through his presence on the field.

Wayne Barnes' tenure as a rugby union referee in the Heineken Cup and European Challenge Cup reflects a pivotal phase of his career, marked by the challenge and prestige of officiating in top-tier European club competitions.

His journey into these tournaments symbolized an ascent to the pinnacle of European club rugby, where he confronted the diversity of playing styles, strategic complexities, and the high-stakes nature of critical encounters.

Officiating in the Heineken Cup, Barnes found himself orchestrating matches that unfolded as grand spectacles of European rugby. From pool-stage clashes to the intensity of knockout rounds, his performances demonstrated an innate understanding of the unique dynamics and pressure points inherent in top-level club competition.

In the European Challenge Cup, Barnes embraced a different set of challenges. This tournament, known for its mix of established and emerging clubs, demanded adaptability. His officiating style mirrored the varied nature of the competition, showcasing an ability to navigate through a diverse array of playing styles and team strategies.

The knockout rounds of these tournaments brought Barnes to the forefront of crucial moments. Whether officiating quarterfinals, semifinals, or finals, he maintained a steady hand in managing the heightened pressure of these encounters. His decisions, often made in the crucible of intense competition, reflected a calm composure and a wealth of experience.

These European competitions were not just stages for rugby matches; they were arenas for defining moments. Wayne Barnes, through his officiating, became an integral part of these moments, influencing the narratives of games with his authoritative decisions, meticulous application of the rules, and an unwavering commitment to fairness.

Beyond the field, Barnes' role in these tournaments contributed significantly to his international recognition. His performances resonated not only with club players and fans but also with the broader rugby community, further solidifying his standing as a referee capable of meeting the exacting standards of top-tier European club rugby.

In essence, Wayne Barnes' officiating in the Heineken Cup and European Challenge Cup represents a chapter where the intricacies of the game met the grandeur of European rugby. His contributions in these competitions not only added to the drama and spectacle but also reinforced his status as a referee capable of elevating the essence of European club rugby through his skill, experience, and unyielding dedication to the sport.

International Referring

Wayne Barnes' involvement in the Rugby World Cup stands as a pinnacle in his illustrious career, marking him as one of the select referees trusted to officiate on the grandest stage of international rugby.

His journey in the Rugby World Cup began with his appointment to officiate matches in the tournament, a testament to his expertise and reliability as a referee. Stepping onto the global stage, Barnes faced the monumental task of presiding over matches that carried the weight of national pride and the pursuit of rugby's most coveted trophy.

Throughout multiple Rugby World Cup editions, Barnes demonstrated a consistent standard of officiating that blended precision, fairness, and an acute awareness of the tournament's high stakes. His role in the tournament extended beyond mere rule enforcement; he became a central figure in shaping the narrative of critical encounters that defined the competition.

The pressure of the knockout rounds, where the margin for error is razor-thin, showcased Barnes' ability to maintain composure and make decisive decisions in moments that often determined the fate of teams vying for glory. The scrutiny at this level is intense, yet Barnes' performances reflected a referee who thrived under the spotlight, ensuring the focus remained on the game itself.

His international contributions expanded to the Six Nations, the Rugby Championship, and the Pacific Nations Cup, further solidifying his reputation as a referee capable of navigating the diverse playing styles and cultures that define the global rugby landscape.

Beyond the technical aspects of officiating, Barnes' involvement in the Rugby World Cup contributed to the tournament's rich tapestry of memorable moments. His decisions, whether awarding crucial penalties or managing contentious situations, became indelible parts of the World Cup narrative, etching his name into the collective memory of rugby enthusiasts worldwide.

As Wayne Barnes continued to officiate on the world stage, his legacy in the Rugby World Cup became a cornerstone of his enduring impact on the sport. His tenure in this prestigious tournament encapsulates a chapter where the passion, drama, and global significance of rugby converged under the watchful eye of a referee who not only understood the game but contributed significantly to its grandest showcase.

Wayne Barnes' role as a referee in the Six Nations Championship underscores his integral position in one of rugby's most prestigious and historic tournaments. His involvement in the Six Nations, an annual competition featuring the national teams of England,

France, Ireland, Italy, Scotland, and Wales, showcased his ability to navigate the complexities of international rugby.

From the outset of his Six Nations officiating career, Barnes found himself in the midst of intense rivalries and passionate encounters that define the essence of the tournament. His appointments to oversee matches in this celebrated competition highlighted not only his technical proficiency but also his capacity to manage the emotional and strategic dimensions that accompany clashes between traditional rugby powerhouses.

Navigating the diverse playing styles of the Six Nations teams required a referee with a nuanced understanding of the sport. Barnes' adaptability and command on the field became evident as he presided over matches characterized by the distinctive rugby cultures of each participating nation. His consistent application of the rules, coupled with an ability to maintain control in high-pressure situations, earned him respect among players and fans alike.

The drama of the Six Nations often unfolded in tightly contested battles that transcended the mere pursuit of championship points. Barnes' officiating decisions, made in the crucible of fervent national rivalries, became integral to the narrative of each tournament. His role extended beyond being an arbiter of the rules; he became a central figure in the ebb and flow of matches that captivated audiences across the rugby world.

As the Six Nations Championship unfolded annually, Barnes continued to be a familiar presence on the field, overseeing critical encounters that shaped the destiny of teams and added to the rich history of the tournament. His contributions to the Six Nations reinforced his standing as a referee capable of managing the grandeur, intensity, and tradition that define one of rugby's most iconic competitions.

Wayne Barnes' officiating in the Six Nations not only exemplified his technical acumen but also solidified his place as a custodian of the spirit and spectacle that makes international rugby, especially within the esteemed context of the Six Nations, a captivating and enduring facet of the sport's legacy.

Wayne Barnes' participation in the Rugby Championship marked a significant chapter in his career as an international rugby referee. The tournament, featuring the national teams of New Zealand, Australia, South Africa, and Argentina, represents a pinnacle of Southern Hemisphere rugby excellence. Barnes' involvement in this prestigious competition showcased his ability to officiate at the highest level of the sport.

As Barnes stepped onto the Rugby Championship stage, he found himself immersed in a cauldron of skill, speed, and physicality. The distinct playing styles of the Southern Hemisphere rugby powerhouses presented a unique challenge, requiring the referee to adapt swiftly to the dynamic and fluid nature of the matches.

His appointments to oversee Rugby Championship fixtures signaled a recognition of his expertise and capability to navigate the nuances of international rugby. The intensity of these encounters, often viewed as a precursor to major international tournaments, demanded a referee who could maintain control while allowing the teams to showcase their formidable skills.

Barnes' role in the Rugby Championship extended beyond enforcing the rules; he became a crucial arbitrator in defining the rhythm and tempo of matches. His officiating decisions played a pivotal role in determining the outcomes of closely contested battles between some of the world's rugby heavyweights.

The pressures of officiating in a tournament of such magnitude were palpable, yet Barnes demonstrated composure and a meticulous approach to decision-making. Whether adjudicating scrums, lineouts, or crucial moments in open play, he consistently upheld the standards of fair play and contributed to the overall spectacle of Southern Hemisphere rugby.

His participation in the Rugby Championship added a global dimension to his refereeing portfolio, as he became a familiar face not only in European competitions but also on the stages where the Southern Hemisphere rugby elite clashed. Barnes' contributions to the tournament underscored his status as an international referee capable of maintaining the integrity of the game at the highest level.

Barnes' involvement in the Rugby Championship showcased not only his technical proficiency but also his ability to seamlessly integrate into the pulsating, dynamic world of Southern Hemisphere rugby. His contributions to the tournament became woven into the tapestry of international rugby, reinforcing his reputation as a referee who could navigate and enhance the spectacle of the sport on a truly global scale.

Wayne Barnes' involvement in the Pacific Nations Cup stands as a testament to his dedication to the global growth of rugby and his role as a referee in fostering inclusivity within the sport. The Pacific Nations Cup, featuring teams from the Pacific region, serves not only as a competition but as a platform for these rugby nations to showcase their talent and compete on the international stage.

In officiating matches within the Pacific Nations Cup, Barnes demonstrated a keen understanding of the unique playing styles and rugby cultures of the participating teams. The tournament, characterized by its fast-paced and expansive brand of rugby, presented a distinct set of challenges that required adaptability and a nuanced approach to refereeing.

Barnes' contribution to the Pacific Nations Cup went beyond the technical aspects of officiating. His presence on the field became a symbol of the global nature of rugby, with a referee of his caliber officiating matches involving teams from the Pacific Islands. His decisions, made with authority and fairness, played a vital role in maintaining the integrity of the competition and ensuring a level playing field for all participating nations.

The significance of Barnes' role in the Pacific Nations Cup extended to the broader context of rugby development in the Pacific region. By officiating matches in this tournament, he contributed to providing these nations with exposure, experience, and an opportunity to compete at an international level. His involvement added credibility to the tournament and highlighted the importance of inclusivity within the global rugby community.

The Pacific Nations Cup, while perhaps not as widely recognized as some other international competitions, held immense importance for the teams involved. Barnes, through his contribution as a referee, became part of the narrative for nations striving to make their mark on the world rugby stage. His experience and expertise served as a valuable asset in elevating the standard of the tournament and contributing to the overall growth of rugby in the Pacific region.

His contribution to the Pacific Nations Cup exemplified not only his technical proficiency as a referee but also his commitment to the principles of fairness, inclusivity, and the global development of rugby. His role in this competition became a reflection of rugby's ability to transcend geographical boundaries and foster a sense of unity and camaraderie among diverse nations within the sport.

Retirements and Impact

Wayne Barnes, the esteemed English international rugby union referee, announced his retirement, marking the end of a remarkable career that spanned various levels of the sport. Born on April 20, 1979, in Bream, Gloucestershire, Barnes had become a recognizable figure in rugby officiating, known for his professionalism, expertise, and significant contributions to the game.

His decision to retire was met with reflections on the legacy he had built throughout his career. Barnes officiated in a multitude of matches, ranging from grassroots competitions to prestigious international tournaments, leaving an indelible mark on the rugby landscape. His retirement signaled the conclusion of a journey that saw him navigate the complexities of the sport, earning admiration for his consistent application of the rules and his ability to manage high-pressure situations on the field.

News of Barnes' retirement prompted tributes from players, coaches, and fans across the rugby community. His impact extended beyond individual matches; it contributed to shaping the broader narrative of rugby, reinforcing the importance of a referee's role in maintaining the integrity and spirit of the sport. His departure from active officiating symbolized the end of an era, prompting reflection on the countless moments he had overseen during his distinguished career.

Throughout his time as a referee, Barnes had officiated in prestigious tournaments such as the Rugby World Cup, the Six Nations, the Rugby Championship, and the Pacific Nations Cup. His retirement represented a transition from an active officiating role to a figure whose influence would persist in the collective memory of the rugby community.

As the final whistle echoed on Wayne Barnes' officiating career, the rugby world acknowledged the significance of his contributions. His retirement served as a moment to celebrate a career marked by dedication, adaptability, and a genuine love for the game. Beyond the technical aspects of refereeing, Barnes left behind a legacy that spoke to the broader impact that individuals, even those behind the scenes, can have on a sport as rich and globally cherished as rugby.

Influence on Rugby Union Refereeing

Wayne Barnes' influence on rugby union refereeing is a narrative woven into the fabric of the sport itself. One of his significant contributions lies in his consistent application of the laws of the game. His ability to interpret and enforce the rules with precision and fairness set a standard for refereeing excellence. Players, coaches, and fellow officials alike recognized his commitment to maintaining the integrity of the sport.

Beyond the technical aspects, Barnes brought a unique demeanor to the field. His composed and authoritative presence under pressure became a hallmark of his refereeing style. This not only contributed to the smooth flow of matches but also set an example for aspiring referees, emphasizing the importance of maintaining control and composure in high-stakes situations.

Barnes' influence extended to the global stage, where he officiated in prestigious tournaments such as the Rugby World Cup, the Six Nations, the Rugby Championship, and the Pacific Nations Cup. His participation in these high-profile competitions showcased not only his individual capabilities but also reinforced the critical role of referees in the narrative of rugby.

The impact of Barnes on rugby union refereeing transcended the field itself. His retirement marked a moment of reflection for the rugby community, prompting discussions on the evolving role of referees and the standards set by individuals like Barnes. His legacy became a touchstone for discussions on the qualities essential for modern referees – fairness, decisiveness, and a deep understanding of the game.

As a mentor and role model, Barnes influenced the next generation of referees. His journey, from local matches to the grand stages of international rugby, became an aspirational narrative for those seeking to officiate at the highest levels. His influence reached beyond the technical aspects of refereeing, touching on the broader aspects of leadership, communication, and sportsmanship.

Barnes' influence on rugby union refereeing is a multifaceted story of professionalism, consistency, and leadership. His legacy is not just in the matches he officiated but in the enduring impact he had on shaping the expectations and standards for referees in a sport that thrives on the principles of fairness, respect, and the pursuit of excellence.

Notable Matches and Moments

Wayne Barnes' refereeing career is studded with notable matches and moments that have etched his name into the annals of rugby history. From local clashes to high-stakes international encounters, Barnes became a central figure in some of the sport's most memorable events.

One of the pivotal moments in Barnes' career occurred during the 2007 Rugby World Cup quarterfinal between England and Australia. His decision to penalize Australia's forward pass in the dying minutes of the match, ultimately leading to England's victory, generated intense debate and scrutiny. This moment, often referred to as the "Giteau incident," exemplified the pressure referees face in critical situations and the subsequent impact their decisions can have on the outcome of a match.

Barnes' involvement in the 2015 Rugby World Cup also left an indelible mark. His handling of the highly contentious pool-stage match between Scotland and Australia drew widespread attention. A last-minute penalty decision awarded to Australia stirred controversy, sparking discussions on the interpretation of the rules. This match highlighted the scrutiny referees face in the age of instant replays and heightened technological analysis.

In domestic competitions, Barnes officiated in numerous English Premiership and European club rugby matches, contributing to the drama and intensity of top-level club competitions. His ability to manage high-stakes encounters in these tournaments further solidified his reputation as a referee capable of handling the rigors of professional club rugby.

Barnes' presence in the Six Nations Championship, one of rugby's premier international tournaments, became a consistent feature. His officiating in matches between traditional rivals like England and France or England and Wales added to the spectacle of the competition, where national pride and historic rivalries often take center stage.

The Rugby Championship, featuring the best teams from the Southern Hemisphere, provided Barnes with the platform to officiate in matches of immense skill and intensity. His contributions to these encounters underscored his adaptability to the diverse playing styles present in the tournament, further establishing him as an international referee of high regard.

Beyond the controversies and high-profile moments, Barnes' notable matches encompass a broader spectrum of rugby. Whether officiating in a local community game or overseeing a World Cup final, his commitment to maintaining the spirit of the game remained a constant. His ability to navigate the intricacies of different competitions and remain a composed figure in the face of intense scrutiny became a defining characteristic of his refereeing legacy.

Wayne Barnes' notable matches and moments form a tapestry that reflects the complexity, drama, and beauty of rugby. His career is not defined solely by contentious decisions but also by the countless instances where his authoritative yet measured approach contributed to the essence and spectacle of the sport.

Conclusion

In the grand tapestry of rugby's history, Wayne Barnes emerges as a pivotal figure, leaving an indelible mark on the sport through his illustrious refereeing career.

Barnes' journey is a narrative of dedication, professionalism, and a deep understanding of the intricacies of rugby union. From local matches in his community to officiating on the global stage, he showcased not only technical proficiency but also an ability to navigate the complexities and nuances inherent in the sport.

His notable matches, including the iconic 2007 Rugby World Cup quarterfinal and the 2015 Rugby World Cup pool-stage clash between Scotland and Australia, became touchstones in the broader conversation about the role of referees in shaping the outcome of matches. Barnes' decisions, scrutinized and debated, reflected the inherent pressure faced by those entrusted with maintaining the integrity of the game.

Yet, beyond the controversies, Barnes' legacy extends to the countless moments where his authoritative yet measured approach contributed to the spectacle of rugby. His involvement in domestic competitions like the English Premiership and European club rugby, as well as his presence in international tournaments such as the

Six Nations and the Rugby Championship, showcased a referee adaptable to diverse playing styles and settings.

What sets Wayne Barnes apart is not only his officiating prowess but also the lasting influence he had on rugby union refereeing. As a mentor and role model, his journey inspired the next generation of referees, emphasizing the importance of fairness, composure, and a genuine love for the game. His retirement, announced with gratitude and acknowledgment from the rugby community, symbolizes the transition from an active officiating role to a legacy that persists in the collective memory of the sport.

Wayne Barnes' contribution to rugby extends beyond the pitch. His career, marked by notable matches, moments of intense scrutiny, and a commitment to the principles of the game, represents a chapter in rugby's narrative where the referee's role is acknowledged and celebrated. Barnes' legacy is not just a collection of decisions; it is a testament to the enduring impact one individual can have on a sport that thrives on its traditions, spirit, and the shared passion of players, officials, and fans worldwide.

Other books written by Thelma Smith

1. MITT ROMNEY; NAVIGATING THE POLITICAL LANDSCAPE

2. THE CHEMICAL BROTHERS; REDEFINING RHYTHM

3. ALAN PATRIDGE; THE EVOLUTION OF A BRITISH COMEDY ICON

4. ARNOLD SCHWARZENEGGER; A LIFE BEYOND LIMITS

5. DOLLY PARTON; HEARTSTRINGS OF AMERICA

6. CHANGING THE NARRATIVE; THE POWER OF JADA PINKETT SMITH

7. SPRINT TO IMMORTALITY; THE UNSTOPPABLE JOURNEY OF DONOVAN BAILEY

8. FROM MOVE IT TO WE DONT TALK ANYMORE; THE CLIFF RICHARD STORY

9. REBEL, ICON, SURVIVOR: THE BOY GEORGE CHRONICLES

10. GEORGE MICHAEL; AN UNFORGETTABLE VOICE

Printed in Great Britain
by Amazon